# Free Concert
*New and Selected Poems*

# Free Concert

*New and Selected Poems*

*by*

Milton Kessler

etruscan press

Etruscan Press
P.O. Box 9685
Silver Spring, MD 20916-9685

www.etruscanpress.org

1234567890

Grateful acknowledgment is made to the editors of
*Artful Dodge* and *Sulfur,* in which some
of the poems in *Free Concert* have appeared.

Publisher's Cataloging-in-Publication

Kessler, Milton.
    Free concert : new and selected poems / by Milton
Kessler. — 1st ed.
    p. cm.
    ISBN 0-9718228-2-4 (HC)
    ISBN 0-9718228-4-0 (PB)


    I. Title.

PS3561.E7F74 2002          811'.54
                           QBI33-648

For my grandchildren

*Aaron, Jonah, Jason, Jordan, Molly, and Mina*

# Contents

### *from* A Road Came Once (1963)

### *from* Sailing Too Far (1973)

## *from* The Grand Concourse (1990)

# Notes on Milt's Way of Working
## (Editor's Note)

I found a letter recently, part of my treasure hoard of Kessler communications, which describes Milt's way of working: "It's Father's Day in Binghamton, USA, mid-June 1989.... I have many new poems that will not be in the book—and my notebooks I know are teeming with all sizes of poetic garments. Here's a tiny poem ["Better"] I wrote a few weeks ago visiting Bertha in the Bronx—jotted it on an envelope." This poem, retitled "Today," reappears as the first poem of *Free Concert*. Milt's words: "This is a complex little validation I guess of my nature—to continue where I am."

The new poems that contribute to this manuscript were part of a folder of possibilities, nestled on top of the piano in the downstairs sitting room/library of 25 Lincoln Avenue (I remember Milt commenting, after thirty years residence in this house, "At least my students always know where to find me"). It was a shared knowledge, Sunni says, that the next book would be collected from the pages of this folder. So we have sifted through these pages—pages typed, penned, penciled, cross-hatched, typed again—with a sympathetic, critical eye, as the work of Kessler demands. Milt was, as he once described his friend Basil Bunting, "historical, skeptical, erotic, insolent" in his writing. He was impulsive and careful, and he listened for the sip of surprise in ordinary conversation; he often worked for years on a single line of a poem, "Yes, word by word." Many of the poems now part of *Free Concert* can be found among his papers in numerous versions, honed from thoughts, notes, letters, and seventy-eight notebooks that are now part of the Kessler manuscript collection to be housed in the Library of Congress. On the day in which Alice Birney, curator at the Library, visited Lincoln Avenue to catalogue and box notebooks and papers, David, Milt's eldest son, discovered an elusive pile of poems, stacked on Milt's "attic-chapel table-top." That night, reading myself to sleep on the Kessler living room sofa (we all met in Binghamton for the first of the Milton Kessler Distinguished Poetry Reader Series), I found, by chance, housed in a nearby bookshelf, another gem, printed in *Sulfur #43*. From this one visit, a meeting of the Kessler clan, five or six poems found their way into the manuscript.

We altered little, and only where clarity demanded, making the best choice of three or four words suspended over a single line in the margin. Milt was intensely aware of the order of poems within a book; he would look or listen for the right riff or sequence of chords as if the composition was jazz. To select, or intuit, the sequence of poems for this book, I spread out poems on the floor of my study like leaves, and over a period of several months, listened for the harmonies, the breeze through the basswood. I watched Milt edit a number of issues of *Choice* magazine; it was an organic process, at once chaotic and methodical. He had a disdain for styles; he loved the many voices that characterize the American language. The result was an eclectic expression representing many, not one. He wrote, watching passengers on a ship bound for Israel, "I read for them...."

I added one word, *will*, to "Plan Book," a poem inspired by a newly found Whitman letter Milt researched. This poem alerts the reader to the enduring bond possible between teacher and student, legacy of Walt and Milt. That bond only grew stronger in the thirty years of our friendship. A poet who writes, in his maturity, "The best times are at night when we sit / in our bathrobes, read and talk....," and "The mind must love the heart...." needs little editing. If the choice was his, we might have fewer poems within this book, but we would be the lesser for it. Even in the squirrel's step from branch to bench, or in the hospital attendant's banter, he could detect the "miracle of the realness." He wrote to me in September of 1993, "Sunni is off to California, Paula, in a few days. Then I will have the whole house to swerve around in and cover with slips of paper." He also wrote: "And what work creation is, the beauty of work." Those slips of paper, often etched with a number 2 pencil, also contain the "lyric lilt of dulcimer, the taste of vowels." Holding his pages, like the heart-shaped basswood leaves that descend to the lawn, we can take pleasure in "the mysteries of the daily ... in the music we share."

Scott Chaskey
Sag Harbor, August 2002

# Foreword

This moving collection of Milton Kessler's last poems—published here together with a selection from his earlier books—begins with tomorrow ("I can read my future in your leaves") and ends in responsiveness to, responsibility for, yesterday ("Why didn't I . . .? / Why didn't I.?") It's a characteristic arc. In person, as in his poems, Milt was a man elated at the forwardness of—the flying unforeseeability of—life itself, and yet, at the same time, a man drawn by heart and instinct back to securer networks of family and history, love and work, networks that bind us, networks that bring the winged singer back to earth.

Whether torn between his sky and his grounding, or putting the two together (as when, in one poem, he stages a scene with "1930 for a sky"), Milt is half Zen master and half Walt Whitman—figures he himself affectionately alludes to. But neither model accounts for the precise dynamic heterosensuality of Kessler's work. "To sing," the second poem tells us, "was the only way through . . . life."

The music of this heartfelt double beat (in and out, down and up, here and there, diastole and systole) is powerfully registered in the new work. To my mind, it comes in the form of two poetic orientations, at first apparently distinct. On the one hand there are stunning spare pulses, say impulses, of formal adventure: long poems made of little pieces; one windpipe of a poem called "Breath" in which repeated units of "this is" and "it is" wrap around an "all" at last—to let the breath out, as the poem ends; and a poem in which "I am nothing compared to . . ." interweaves again and again with its alter ego "I am nothing to compare to." (Formally the powers of this latter poem arise not only from its subtle variation-on-a-sameness, in that long list of parallel constructions, but also from the varieties of noun-things that pile up after the "I am nothing"s, to complicate the sure refrains with wowing unpredictabilities.) These poems dare to broach cooler terrains than some earlier ones did, terrains of spirit from which even a heart's heat cannot save us.

*xiii*

On the other hand, there is the continuing force of Milt's old themes, particularly themes of nature, work, and love—all of them sharpened and darkened slightly by mature experience. "Geese fly in the valley of ashes / Looking like a stream" is not, after all, entirely unrelated to "After I was fired I thought about mountains. / Rehired I was angry and walked around the block." "Work Song 1980" is nothing if not a love song. (Whenever thinking threatens to think itself the founding member of the free-love society, it is chastened into wisdom: "He was the pupil of her eye. / That certainly is a pretty plant. / This terrace is worth the rent. / The mind must love the heart.") The songs for Sonia, the marriage poems, are particularly touching: after decades of marriage, they find themselves able to "surprise themselves together."

Perhaps a posthumous collection always seems prescient. The fact that Milt, in the years of these last, new poems, attended so many sickbeds and deathbeds leaves its poignant signature here. "Hospital Conversation" seems to record a casual exchange between nurse and patient, yet deepens into a kind of kindness native to Kessler's sensibility. He was a man for whom the memory of emerging from the movies in 1995 is a celestial memory: recorded as a series of simple questions, it holds forever his childlike elation at the simple evidence of the senses, in the face of a breathtakingly unexpected, utterly unshaded, moon.

Heather McHugh

# Free Concert
*New and Selected Poems*

# Free Concert
*New and Selected Poems*

# Today

All these years, tree,
you have been growing from the sidewalk.

Now you are right beside my 5th floor window,
where I can read my future in your leaves.

# Tiny Flashlights
*Always*

To sing was the only way through High School and life:
thanks to choral master Scudder, thanks to God and my
father for the bass-baritone I had for my Bar Mitzvah,
the DeWitt Clinton choir, Wilhowsky's All City High Chorus,
and my greatest day ever (even greater than my afternoon
with Frost)—Eleanor Roosevelt's visit, 1944, Herald
Tribune Forum, Waldorf Astoria, where I sang, one of four
schoolboy basses from the five boroughs, photo in the
*New York Times* in suit and tie, "The Battle Hymn of the
Republic," Christ was born for you and me across the sea,
and she shook my hand. Years later, saved by the Temple
Israel choir in Buffalo, saved by the Handel and Haydn
Society in Boston, "Messiah," "Sanctus Civitas," the old man
Williams, there. At the Met I didn't sing but walked
with spear, flute, flagon, cape, beside Rise Stevens,
Baccoloni of the seven napes and vast Lawrence Melchoir.
At fifteen, my hero, Giovanni Martinelli, rang.

My teacher, Florence Turitz Bower, was rich on Central Park
West. I lay on her carpet and breathed and sweated, her
fingers on the buttons of my shirt, my larynx approved by
a physician. I saw the chords myself in his mirror. Drink
to me only with thine eyes, over and over to be free in
the muzzle as I would never be, but how could she know. I
was very good looking then—dropped out of school and

4

shining with fantasy and fragmentation or masturbation.
Even Frederich Shaur, Wagnerian bass-baritone of the Metropolitan,
his friends in the back row, I sang for him,
shivering, then he for me, and said I might one day sing
heroic tenor I remember or did I invent it? Did it happen?
What happened? All the roles I sang, the solitary concerts I
conducted with tiny flashlights. Oh rescue yourself with
song, my boy, rescue yourself with song. And of

how Josef Krips struck his breast and cried, Now you
see your God, and I leaped into "Ode to Joy" as if the
greatest German music could save a Jewish boy.

# Careers

My father didn't want to be a foreman;
his fellow workers were his friends:
the night-shift, parcel post, GPO.

My Aunt Anne's first job
lasted a lifetime:     ZOA,
Palestine Supplies.

My wife became a teacher,
never wanted to be a principal.
Third grade, fifth grade.

My mother finally
got work during WWII
and had money. She has one child.

Before and after
the ice cream parlor
my grandpa peddled newspapers.

Uncle Bernie played handball,
my Uncle Lou, baseball, both
worked in the Post Office too.

Lou is dead. His kid brother
just turned seventy. Poetry has nothing to do
with getting ahead.

# Zarafshan

No. Poetry is a place
   grand rivers disappear in sand.
  It leaves no gold linen at all
    except what a bird's backbone

              knows to follow.

# Good Friends/Rhetorician

You have lived too long
to enter the room of your thoughts.
Stay out here and write what you see.

I am tired of looking outside
and finding graphic lies and illusion.

"These I drive away
with the hand of my heart
from the face of my remembrance."

Now I will look inward only
at the radiant shades of emptiness.

# Many Sides to the Moon

I need to call

    for the care
      these years of work
were for.

      I can't help myself,
The times of busyness

    are twisting
    into something slow.

I need you
to read

    with me,

      now.

# Moshe Ben Avraham Living Alone
## Gives Last Instructions to His Children

Children, All my life
        I was not careful of cleanliness.
        Your mother complained I didn't bathe
        for three weeks after the marriage which told her
        what life would be like with me and she was right.

        Sometimes, I wouldn't wash my mouth for months
        and would touch a woman's silk with unclean hands
        and smell like a trough in my clothes and woke
        to remember my father's feet grisly
        through torn blankets in daylight
        and my mother's nightly grief.

        Only on Holydays did I dress like a mensch,
        my wardrobe a rag-gatherer's chest of dust-drenched mold.
        Nobody called as I wheezed my days away, shuddering
        at refreshment, "too cold, too hot," like an infant
        until my hair and sex glare like Les Halles,
        my head glinting in the slaughterhouse basket
        for want of pleasure.

When I die, dear children, honor your royal descent.
Take Moshe Ben Avraham from his naked box, drip
and scrub him in rainwater at last, wrap him
in white cotton and white socks,
                              behind
his neck a nice tallis and white pillow
filled with cool fine sand.
                    Thus,
God willing, he will feel a freshness
in death, better than the cold blood of birth
better than the burning urine of life.

# Our Immortality

When you say goodbye to part of yourself
that life doesn't ever die

though you will no longer follow it.
We only follow some side of ourselves

and we must say goodbye over and over.
So remember, they are not dead the ones

you said goodbye to. They keep trying
invisibly within us, a secret shining

you know as weeping that sometimes comes
between us and those we would love.

# Breath

This is
It is
It is
This is
It is
This is
This is
It is
It is
This is
It is
Is
This is
It is
It is
is
is
It is
It is
Is
This is
All
It is

# Half-Century Passengers

My friend is reading Shakespeare
preparing for his classes.

He is peaceful with    pipe and glasses,
marking passages and margins,
leaves slowly swirl around him.

We might share    confusions at noon,
but why disturb such a human scene.

Leaves slowly swirl around him,
marking passages and margins
marking passages and margins.

# Remembrancing Dancing in 5J

Pop, you are not tiptoe
        hanging up your blue wool sweater
and your lips
        are not sipping a sweet cup of coffee
and your daily paper
        who is cursing it
and your chair
        who is keeping it honest
and your ashtray
        never leaves the shelf above the sink
and your suit
        who is wearing it in the street
and your Ludens coughdrops
        who is savoring them
        Under your tweed hat
        I am saving them
        and your pocket pencil
        inside with them
        and your privacy
        safe among them
and who will say
        as we skip at the doorstep:
Well, Milton, you're always welcome.
You got the ocean, you got the beach,
you got the boardwalk. You got the terrace.
You can rest and recoup the strength you lost.

# Scales

The prairie is more roiling higher

and plains
flat wheat and bison.


This double harp inside your heart
striving

for the shaking.


Two diesels pull, three diesels push,
catheter-red gondolas
into mountain
chimney.


Out of the maze we punch out
our cartouche
onto frozen mud.
Plain, ornate, it's mated-maze made.


Ladder, I earned my back today.
Ladder, I earned my chains today.
Ladder, I earned my bed.

The child runs fast from great grand
mother who can't catch up

but it stops.


Dieto cracked his hirpled leg
                    to die
posing as a flower pausing.


"I was a cross-handed hitter, kid,


                    strong
        to the opposite field."


How, Bertha said,
can I make you happy?
I don't have any money.


Now the hollow basswood's down.
If we live through winter, wife,
Oh let us
            grant thy garden.

Mao, dementate, "Pupils obey!
　　　　Bring
two dead sparrows
to school a day."


Last bed should be a beach
　　　your great grandchild waits

so two can reach.


Cinders and sparklers
　　　on sills and rails.
A nightshift ferry seething into its birth.
Cablights frame avenue, street, rain.


Over own open baritone jaws near
saw Ralph Vaughn Williams ear
　　　Golden City premier.

# Work Song: 1980

He drove slowly past her school,
the little blue car tiptoe in its numbered spot,

thought of her teaching in that pleasant seeming building,
smoke crayoned on the windless sky, people going
about life in some orderly October fashion.

His mind hurt with tears of need for her and envy.

Her car looked like a nice new pair of shoes
or slippers in the foyer of a party
to which he had been forbidden.

Something was coming too clear,
and he swerved into the sleep of the late morning.

His partner in reality
he had lost her.

# Primary

Lemon shirt, blue jeans,
flash of tiny toes
warm against
grandma's own
afghan.

Fresh Negev dust
at sliding door. . . .

Hand to hand
flax of Jewish hair
white walls
boy in
red chair.

\*

As she plays cards the perfect girl,
with yellow willow buds in her hair,
tan knees astride under her
white dress edged red, sandals
outspread, as she rocks
on her strong ankles,
and I see in starlight,
Shulamite, the Bride. . . .
She is merely nine, the boy eight.
I turn then to the sands
of Beersheva and write:
"Our neighbor's daughter come to play.
Her new blue bike outside
celebrates her birthday."

# In Winter, the Door Makes a White Rainbow

A man and a woman
living out the death sentence of marriage?

I don't care for my own ways
but to live interdependently true.

Oh suffering is not the same as death,
loss of dream and gift not same as death
loneliness is not the same as death
failure not same as death.

A plum is not a dark woman.
Brooklyn cherry blossoms are cherry blossoms.

And what do they know of love
who would rather a mortal of ghosts?

"Oh I feel so good," dying Whitman said
Mickle Street house under his head
in his makeshift water bed.

A plum is not a dark woman.

A mairu, completely depend on you. Thanks,
thank you.

Sonia, from whom thrice came more holy fabric
than wind and moon and star send back, return from the separateness
de Tocqueville called democracy. See the waxwings burst burst burst,
surprise themselves together on the reaching branch again.

# Riding First Car:
## *Learning the Boxes*

:

A man with a fast heart
rests on a hill in a grass jacket
and gilt hat flower,
face facing bursting light.

:

The flowered armless chair
rides next to the armed solid one.

:

As toy cathedrals the migrants dig
their daily coin.

Circus trucks wait
to pick up the dark backs.

:

To lie far from your lamp corner
in a chasm of falling thoughts
and the mist above them.

:

Shy and stiff-thighed at the party
left profile colder than right

goes from stranger to stranger.

:

Do people ever sit here, she says.
    It's a nice spot.

Oh yes, he says.

:

These leaves and buds have keyways passwords
for every twisting gust of breaking out beside
masts, buttresses and russet bells of giant firs.

:

A woman with a bruised eye and cracked glasses
settles in and sugars her coffee.

:

I notice down there I'm wearing
van Gogh's boots.

Who put them on
my twisted yellow feet?

:

Why waste the food, he says,
waving the tray away.

:

See, there's a miniature dinosaur
in the sidewalk, a winged one, asleep,

                    a bird in asphalt.

:

After the "little ice age" and Crusades
for three years it rained hard rain: 1315–17 CE,
irrigated the plague.

They blame the dry Jews.

:

Bertha mentions Belle. Your sister is still
with you? she says. No, Betty says.
She has been gone for six years, a long time.
They sit quietly under the Sabbath lights.

                              Both ninety.


:


Piers and rails and tanks and barges and steam
and shacks and trucks and here and there
a speck with two legs on cement
and 1930 for a sky.


:


It is soon Spring

and trees are still mated
to sidewalk gray ice
inside the woods.


:


On the island after supper
she stepped out and took this picture
lit by the click of her new gift camera
these nightsea stars.


:

A moon pursuing the couch
and sweater of heather.

:

Ice doesn't want to give way
but it's done what it can

for the play.

:

Having thermos tea and cookie,
    nearby a squirrel eating lunch
        I hold my tea with both hands
            and leap from bench to bench.

:

:

:

:

"We have so many things to talk about," she says,
after the afternoon
            in the park,
"but there isn't any air," she says.

:

2 men eating lunch on a girder
       35 floors up
talking in the sky and smiling.

:

A blind grandmother binds on her shawl
stands and looks
    toward the platform door.

:

The running watch is closing in
on the stopped clock

Look, now it passes
and for a time es-capes.

:

Poor woman walking in winter
so dim the teeth show in rows
beneath cheek-skin.

:

They called and said,
"Get up and put on your uniform."

So I got up
and had breakfast,

then went back to my body.

:

Oh what nice rolls.
They really give you
your money's worth.

:

You get rest by sleeping when you are tired
no matter where that is.

You take rest when the need rises,
as mammals do.

:

Geese fly dark in the valley of ashes
looking like a stream.

:

After I was fired I thought about mountains.
Rehired I was angry and
                    walked around the block.

:

Crown against the windshield
and gold carpaint for a bed
my line is Nowhere River
and shoes rot red.

:

See we've run out of the tunnel.
These weeds touching the train    are green,
just like
            in the country.

:

This worry attacks my waking,
disabling the robe of day.

:

A bearded man in the mirror,
seeing his yellowed underwear
      and a synagogue burning far.

:

I can't cheer at the opera as in old times
but twist and wrench
against the bindings of my chair.

:

He wrapped his clay statue in his only blanket
and froze to death beside it in Paris 1864.


:


The couple on the West End Line,
her on his shoulder, his shined shoes split,
their little tartan suitcase crumpled
her purse in his lap.


:


This time of year
if the sun is out
there's no better
        weather.


:


He was the pupil of her eye.
That certainly is a pretty plant.
This terrace is worth the rent.
The mind must love the heart.


:


Girl,
holding her hand in her lap like her child.


:

It would have been nice to have the family together,
tuned to the time before we were born.

:

They are sleepy and clean and trusting
the old bridge girders to Brooklyn.

# Lullaby

The last time I saw my grandmother
I was angry on the subway.

All these years
I can't remember why.

But when she got off I said or thought
something nasty. Had she nagged me?

Who knows what is important
to a boy of twelve.

No one was there except for the strangers—
and could I have been going on alone?

This story I've told myself
all my life long.

The last time I saw my grandmother
I did something wrong.

# Shalom Chaverim

He looks up to me and says
soon I'm going to take
a long trip on a train
way into the country.

That's a good idea I say.

Then he looks up to me lighter and says
soon I'm going to take a light trip
on a train
        way into the mountains.

That's a better idea I say.

Then he looks up to me
            much lighter
and says sooner I'm going to take
        a longer trip
    on a very light train
        way into the sky.

That's a brilliant idea I say

and we kiss and ride.

# Conversation

I like your hair ribbon, he said,
          very colorful this morning.
I love towels too, she said,
     rolling him over.
Buy more without even
            needing them.
I like to open the closet and see them
      neat and bright
        and to feel how soft
    a new towel is.
He took his injection
     and smiled at the sky.

# Plan Book

The leaves of the southern shrubs
lift and shiver
in the balmy Sunday.
3 pm seems like the time eternity holds to.
Lazy June is the poet's time of rest.
Sweet sun on your neck speaks
and mountains smooth up to the cumulus.
The battlefields are mown and the spared grass
tangles the fence lines.
Lean against your green car's trunk
and think of paralyzed Walt
a hundred years ago today.
"Was took out 2 hours Saturday, horse and wagon,
to a pleasant quiet waterside shore. Best love to you,
$2 enc'd, W.W."

        Students,

        On this
        hill
        we will
        meet again:
        100 years

        Password:
        Walt Whitman.

# Homage

This man disinfecting wall and floor
              does it well
       though no one oversees
                            or supervises.

       With rag and mop
                     he polishes
              corners and appearances
        for the next poor framed
                            passenger unnamed.
And as he cleans
              we speak
       of the shining house
                     he owns.

# Love, S

"The luminescence of, no, the translucency
                              of the living."

"To love is to trust someone
                    into your translucence."

I see
what they don't see.

But they have
what I don't have

and
I know it.

Such a month, since the nice
note from Sonia, 8/7/91,

Hi Milt,
welcome home—
hope the trip was good—
I'll be back early
Friday eve.
Looking forward to shabbat
and new career.
Love, S

# Comma of God

I am nothing compared to the Medicaid sneer
I am nothing compared to the owner of the door
I am nothing compared to the elevator of Heidegger
I am nothing compared to the spokes of Vincent's Belgian sunflower
I am nothing compared to Rodin's least mistress
I am nothing compared to the frames of Hamlet
I am nothing compared to a critic or chauffeur
I am nothing compared to my old fire engine
I am nothing compared to the breasts I see
I am nothing compared to a tree in any season
I am nothing compared to the escalator of Duchamp
I am nothing compared to Maronetti's future
I am nothing to compare with Turner's clouds
I am nothing to compare with the lens of Claude
I am nothing to compare with my mother in 1930
I am nothing to compare with the cockroach in the drain
I am nothing to compare to the jew-haters' snot
I am nothing compared to the beak or bill
I am nothing compared to the past or the present
I am nothing to compare with any suit on the rack
I am nothing to compare to a loaf or child
I am nothing to compare with any syllable of Homer
I am nothing to compare with the foot of a chair
I am nothing to compare with the truth of your anger
I am nothing compared with what I failed to do
I am nothing compared with one note of Lester Young
I am nothing compared to the images of Vietnam

I am nothing compared to the furnace of Dresden
I am nothing compared to the last drops of snow
I am nothing compared to a bicycle with wings
I am nothing compared to the comma of God

# Selected Random Sayings by Kosho Shimizu
## Chief Abbot, Todaiji

Flesh deepens spirit. Spirit stings flesh.

Freedom? Try walking.

The dissatisfactions of a happy man, what's more difficult?

Mud on your hands? Sit. Eat.

Don't fight it.

Gold is gold. Silver is silver. Lead is lead.

Cedars in a mountain. Sweetfish in a brook.

Saying anything perfectly? Impossible.

Straight searching is good. Loitering on the way is fragrant.

You have to forgive me.

Once you realize it, it's simple.

There are good days and there are fair days.

A good good, lucky one. A lucky, good good one.

See, even in me there is something good.

To exist is very strange.

Stepping down, be careful, know yourself.

We have been thinking this or that for ten thousand years.

                              Today is best.

He complains, and enjoys the sound.

*Translated by Milton Kessler & Tateo Imamura*

# Accompanied

*"Paintings are not properly seen in galleries
but only in the solitude and wholeness of their studios."*
Pousette-Dart

Hush. On    whitewashed wall
a huge furry moth
the color of mammal
sleeps through noon and tomorrow.

My large stomach and sides pain
and I need to see a doctor
but rain is driving even sparrows
into high grass hiding     and ground
cannot swallow the sky-gift pooling.
Now it is bones that ache
as I move my shoulder    painting rain.


Poor God, we are sick and tired,
so I'll build us a glass of tea.

The four frightened sisters lie
hand in hand
on an iron bed in Brooklyn.
Only Berry, a mother, still wakes.

When you have nobody
it inhibits travel.
Like the soul you linger
by the freed dead body.

Passing 24 tiles of sunshine
on scoured corridor wall,
the buttressed windows
sealed and webbed.

# Joan at the Golden Grill

Was I afraid to show myself
even after she coaxed me?
And her live hair so gracious
on my face
that I had to mention
why I was frozen
so long.
"You won't believe this," I said,
"but it's because of my gray hair."
I didn't tell her
that I sensed
the girls would be ashamed
to dance
with all my evidence
in front of others
under the grinding sparklers.
Did I know
that everyone danced
in a rainbow?
Thus I hesitated to be invited
and with her hand she did.
"You're beautiful, Joan.
Your hair is very beautiful."
"You're a good dancer," was her answer.

# Sketching Pain on Lincoln Avenue

We watch him gently move the chessmen
from their formal tiny towns

huddling them forever
each a part of the touching party.

Kings, Queens, Knights, Pawns:
each a part of the touching party.

"What's the matter?" the wind said.
"It's all wrong," the shoulder answered.

Each a part of the touching party.
It's a part of the touching party.

# Dancing Lesson

Each daybreak I reach to take medicines
    losing balance
                at the edge of her bed.
     Then bend to polish
           jewels
       in the kitchen
             sink
and send up
         mist of coffee to her
         and settle
   with my bowl of grains.
Only after I've finished
    does she rub her bad knee
    and descend
   to the oval oak table
  and calendar
     of today.

Here by the one sunny window I read,
  *The Tsurezuregusa of Kenkō:* 1330–1332
   "The Holyman of Kume lost his magic power
   to fly after noticing the legs
    of a girl washing clothes."
I watched a woman hanging sheets
  on a windy roof in the Bronx.

They were white as

                            painted feet

    of Asian slaves
on sale in Rome.

# New Month

Walk toward the epicenter of leaves on grass
struggle to  keep carrying  heavy bones
as I must  each biblical day
  far from any bench
and without breath   Exhale   Expire
Sonia watches from a distant table   reads.

I failed to find help in the tools of poetry. When asked
  what was wanted,
      fell into deafness-rain.
    Pain became
      frozen reason.

To make up for the years without you, reader, I hug
      suffering and illness
which comfort me like the shoulders of a sweet roll
                              at Reznikoff's.

Glassdoor opens
          and sunlight stands in the room,
competing with  blankness.
"Who are you," she says,  irritable
that balance is challenged.
"I am ice," it says, "the origin of things."
It starts to climb and she follows, melting as they descend.

He rubs his embedded fingers as I write as if
                    he was making
        fire,
    faster and faster he swirls them,
              a beggar
rolling a warm nut.


How can I leave you, reader, just having found you again
in your corner-seat, empty pages shaking.

But I have an appointment with sleep.
No rimes left for subway souls.


               Wife worked hard today
baking and laundry. Her legs cold
as she goes to bed.　Pull quilt over
     her shoulder.
        Go down to pay debts.
Nov.1, '99　We　51 yrs
                  this season.

# Not Yet Two

My grandson Jonah is holding an apple
the color of his shirt and lips.
We see two apple faces
friends for a thousand years.
Yes, this instant lasts longer than a lifetime.
Paper is durable after all.
Even more so than trees.


"Do you want to come in?  I'll light
the candles," she says, "it's the last night."


"I'll be right in," he says,
writing down what she said.


After many years of wasting my life
in poems no one wanted, my worthless work,
my operatic pretense and false compassion,
I find myself silent among the famous
at David Ignatow's memorial
where I am told by his mistress that she was glad
I appeared there, because "he held your work
in very high regard."

Do you want to say the prayers, she says.
Let's do it together, he says.
After he prays alone, they stand
before the 8 candles, separate as Adam and Eve
after their wedding in Eden.

# After the Movies: 1995

Is that the moon?

I've never seen
the moon so close.

Can you believe it?

That's a solid object
in the sky.

Can you imagine?

Is the moon
new or full?

Is the full moon
just one day?

Is the moon
the whole moon?

Moon. Moon?

# Poetry Is the Most Enduring of All the Arts

I wondered what this wetness was
on my bed as I turned
back the quilt and smoothed the crumpled
sheet.
I felt the drops of milk, it was milk,
my son's milk or my daughter-in-law's milk.

They were miles down
the road with the babies
as I tasted it and lit
the temple of the night.

# Esplanade for HB

With Jewish eye
*look at magical worlds.*
Moses knew a figure
*of being unlike Rothko.*
Glazing graze, cattle camel,
*the heat of the secret.*
When living tree burns green
*figure survives fire.*
Colors of waiting to meet Mamma,
*prayer, solitaire.*
Stores of study, bridge tables, piano branch,
*bench, study of store.*
Evening rose under holding leaves,
*woman's soul behind wood.*
Menorah, clearing by temple,
*places of trees by streams, lost names.*
Oh dressed and nothing doing in the cards,
*not father's favorite.*
Mammals and roots to barn,
*artist guarding mother, rest east.*

# Delight

Now that I can make nothing
acceptable to myself
I love my old things
when I can find them
in attic trunks & boxes, but
even then, how does this memory
compare to the face of
little Jonah holding an apple
with his delightful fingers.

Suddenly, the sweetness of the paper rose
touched me bending over my coffee.
I looked up for the first time
at its most perfect pleasure
in the music we share.

# Amidah
## Euphorbia Abyssinica: Pebbles That Bloom

: Native to the southern African deserts, these minimal plants
    Lord open my lips and my mouth shall praise
: Take on a pebble-like appearance
    Thou sustain the living with loving kindness
: That camouflage them from thirsty animals
    Praised are thou O Lord
: Notice how close to the ground they grow, exposing
    Thou call the dead to immortal life
: A minimum of surface to the drying sun and wind
    Thou keep faith with those who sleep in the dust
: Daylight needed for synthesis enters each plant
    Holy are thou and holy is thy name
: Through small window-like places
    Thou causes the wind to blow and the dew to form
: The remaining surface reflects light. Once
    Holy Holy Holy our mouth will speak praise
: A year these unattractive members
    Thou did choose us for thy service
: Of the carpet-weed family must
    Loving us and taking delight in us
: Burst into attractive bloom
    Remember us, this day, save us.

Ailanthus Altissima: China

: Earth still gives me joy!

:            See

:                              that butterfly

:                          just going around

:              over the moss and

:                          roots

:                  of The Tree of Heaven.

*from*

# A Road Came Once
*(1963)*

# To Paul, for the Passage

Paul, father, to have known you,
to have seen you wince and turn your head,
to have shared your table, to have seen
your secret dignity, your candleflame of pride,
live in the dim corners, with papers and radios,
in hallways and hospitals, was to have ascended
a Zion of vision. To have seen
your cancered hope survive, father of quiet joys,
of walks and lovely faces, what other miracle
can we know in life, we, the insignificant,
the congregation of subway faces.

Paul, father, there are only a few of us;
we are a small family, but we are enough.
We have shared a troubled life;
there has been little time for peace.
Now rest. It is a beautiful day.
The grass is not cold.
The ground is alive.

# The Lynching

Dragged through doorways of fragrance
Dense as embalmer's perfume, Parker,
Wounds deep as blossoms,
Died beneath magnolia.
He fell; then sky was
Grass, and the flash of quartz in stone.
Blood soured; the cage was not enough.
They hacked the white bones through.

Tonight, in Poplarville,
The rain dies at the eaves;
Leaves fall face-downward;
The hill-shacks breathe on their stones;
Porches sag like lips
Tasting blood in their corners;
And three men sit on a fence
Only their odors alive.

But it happened, then, there,
With flowers: jasmine, lily, magnolia;
And by the smell of flowers
He knew the place.
Now, beneath birds,
Licked by the water's drifting mold,
Parker, skin bleaching white,
Swells in the Pearl River.

# Hymn to the Rain

This day is glorious with rain.
Men sift for home in mist
To sing from windows, deep as graves,
Their sea-bird hymns.

This day is glorious with rain.
Women break their witches' knots
And go within to lamps and bread.
Now the benches are cleansed;
The dowager elms
Bow down with reverence.

O this day is glorious with rain.
I cannot vulture in my books today.
I must warm the salt-sea with my bones.
I will run beneath the blackest cloud;
There will I lie, with the youngest grasses,
And lick the nipples of rain.

# The Clerk Retires

Fog infects the entrance of the house,
suffocates the lights like summer flies.
Sick, he breathes the pallid city dawn,
trembles like an ancient closet-moth,
incapable and blind.
                    Now he rubs
the smoothness of his hands, listens
to the knock of heat in walls, and chants:
I have fingered forty years of letters,
written picture postcards in the summers;
now I'll sing; I'll do many things.

Then he closed the shades, and dressed,
washed his hands again, and left, fresh
as a turned collar.  Avoiding ice,
he took the alley, followed by dogs,
and went downtown.

In the subway, the breast of a shop-girl
touched him. He could feel it, there,
against his arm. It was the first time
in years. He felt sick, then, standing
in an overcoat and rubbers.

At the cafeteria, the same strangers sat
four to a table, quiet, as if in separate grief.
He had a good seat. He could see, in the window,
the paper garden. Flowers leaned, in the glare,
painfully, awkwardly, like ghosts of his mother.

Nine o'clock,
but there was no work that day. He walked.
The traffic drenched his feet with cold.
He went to the lunch-place, too early;
without the others, they never knew his face.
Stiff, ashamed, a small man at the edge of a chair,
he ate another breakfast.

The reading room was warm. He slept,
in magazines and papers, all day.
Time to go home, the guard said.
He woke, feverish, still
in his overcoat and rubbers.
He went to the washroom.
The icy water was too wonderful.
He died there.

# The Squatters

All week the wreckers disembowel the street;
a hundred years of faces shake to sand.
The concrete trudgeon takes their breath away;
they cough the plaster on their splintered porch.
"Go in," he says, "the air is bad today."

Inside, they smell the orange heater-gas,
the drafts that flush and rash their son to chills.
Another building stumbles to its mouth. . . .
The mirror sways; it brings him to the wall—
all fractured glass, asthmatic, rotting tooth,
a jell-eyed, balding thirty.

Yet, still a child, he hugs against his wife;
and as they walk their cubicles like ghosts,
his nine month cloistered fetus, jarred,
leans forward, blue, and prayerfully.

# The Long Friends

She finds a brilliant in a waste of sand;
With dignity she sanctifies the stone.
Her face is cradled in the lap of moss;
The grass is cool as her mother's hand.
With gentleness she reads a fern.
She listens to a moving worm.
Come to me worm, she says.

She mumbles it forward.

# Beyond Anguish

At dawn, caught beneath the rim of light,
it fled into a place still black,
tore its side upon a nail,
and bled small robes upon the snow.
Then rain came, and fever, then cold
and the long cool drowse.
It slept to death within the cling of ice,
curled on its side in fetal dreaming.

At evening, when cobblestones shiver,
and every path has a figure,
the dead leaves jump in a flash of wind,
the trees are black with holding on.
And here in the snow he finds it,
under a window of laughing faces.
He thinks it is a child stillborn.
In anguish, he follows his own breath home.

But this night, the air changes, the bird comes,
men gather to smell the springtime.
And warm with thaw the gray fur shifts
equal in wind with the yellow grass.

# Anniversary Poem

We raged again last night.
Your wail pierced my skull
until my tongue was
bloodless, white, and locked
against my teeth like stone.
In a whale's panic, I shook,
struck, broke your sound.
Then we lay breathless,
grotesque, like swollen puppets.

Last night, we made another son.
Today, cool, affecting ease,
we walk, tall as our skeletons.
Yet, beautiful are these bones;
in the body of our son see them.
And for the loneliness
that we still share in pain,
and for the face
that you have given him,
I, fleshed and hairless,
my own father now,
give you my boyhood still.

*from*

# Sailing Too Far
*(1973)*

# Flight Marker I

Myrtle, Woodbine, Appletrees, Trillium,
here they are.   The strength of your arm
stalls at the open gate of the stars.

Feel everything, trust everything!

Venus calls from her dream of earth.
I dream her perfect sleeping oriental face,
her certainty of sexual grace. No storm
flaws her mating with that vast wisdom of the moon.

Feel everything, know everything!

That fragile hope of my uncovered skull
smothers with empty words of bliss. . . .
I am small in this bright cataract of pine.
I stand on the smallest stone.
I am a standing prairie dog
praying for my song.

# Lost Song

When the wind in the mosaic pool
shimmered the pebbles as bells
I walked on the blades of shells
and pruned the prickly roses.

When the circlets of ruby beads
braided my fingers with wine
I knelt at the knees of the wind
shadowed in sand as a vine.

In the eye of the wind was a woman
white as a dream of oblivion
crooked at the knees of her son
touching his feet with her hair.

# A Boy

Out there a boy
is watering roses.
He holds a long, twisting black hose.
The bushes are frightened.
The flowers
enduring
shiver his noisy coaxing.
It's all right
though, they say,
reassuring.
We know him.
He is gentle,
and, besides,
his long, red shirt, flapping,
entertains us.

# The Passing Bell

I'll go now
nuzzling
my infant son.
How he warms
against me
in the harbor shower,
how his heart
kicks bravely
the passing bell.
My own ribs
shiver—
this evening rain.
Danny Danny,
the friends are mine.
*They cringe with laughter*
*my mind's away. . . .*
The sand is loam,
the harbor mild,
the old scows dirge,
the dawn-wind comes.
Ebb tide:
gull faces
squall
in the rocks.

# Letter

So they too lecture us on how to live and feel.
Well, they're right, I guess.
My sickness, this halting monolith
of sullen dust I scrape and shave; today,
this face, these stalled eyes,
a mother could not make them weep.
The world passes a doomed face.

It is quite different here this time,
and not surprising, after everything.
Blind, angry, haunted, my windows call
and drench me in my chair; the air is dead
and deep, the breath of my own blessing falls.
These friendships die of love.  Fired, we move again,
we move again, again. . . .

O now, there, about us, silent, innocent,
in their own sweet dreams I pray for them,
the leaves, our broken days, descend and gather.
O I'm tired, wife, my mind is late October in the ditch.
Forgive me, I will not call. Live, live,
while I'm away, and David, Paula, fair Daniel,
my father Arthur, my mother Elizabeth, take care;
and you, wife, you are a good woman,
you have nothing to be ashamed of, do you hear,
nothing to be ashamed of, no matter what I've said.

# The Willow Songs

## 1

This girl, whose hair I dream,
walks like a willow in an endless dawn.
There is no harm in her. She is innocence adrift.
There is no school for her, no work at all.
We call her tragedy. The time loves nothing better.
Lord, let her move among thy searing highways
without shame or grief. Let no gold rapist
soil her sorrow. Her name is dreams,
my neighbor's truant daughter.

## 2

I met my mother
at the station.
Everywhere
were Sabbath faces.
Golden children
clapped the Hora,
fern and ivy
breathing *Mazel.*
There we danced
and danced again,
whirling willows
in the rain.

Thunder knelt
and drove me back:
"The Sabbath Queen,
the Sabbath Bride."


3


Where have I come
unknown to me before?
The stone door widens.
The stars move close.

My house is better,
wondrous and mild.
My children dance
for the joy of it.

To rise! To rise!
To sing all day.
Home in the willows.
Home in the rain.

Give me now
my woman to love.
My first woman,
my homely wife.

# American Voices: *Late Twentieth Century*

I'm happy. What I do now is my own business.
The old couple, brother and sister, crowd
beside me, as if I were their own black son.
We're frightened.
I look too long at her rose bronze face,
her ivory blouse,
and turn away with pleasant shame.
She is a beautiful color.
And as I show her the white cloud cover over
the frozen great lake, she leans against me.
We help each other. It is our first flight together.
Clouds above us, clouds under us,
we tell our stories. She is from Georgia,
a southern lady, a spinster.
We share the black coffee and the long wait
and change in Chicago, a terrible city,
so many awful homes. My face feels better.
My lover, we are perfect strangers.
It's springtime there you know, she to a
funeral in Los Angeles, I to San Diego
to read old poems.
Clouds above us, clouds beneath us.
O dark mother I confess; yes, I have dreamt
bad subway dreams about your sisters' breasts—
or were they always bad?

I'm happy. What I do now is my own business.
It's been nice. The happy mourners, brothers! sisters!
we come down. They take each other's arm and frown and
   go.
They proudly say "goodbye."

# The Rant of the Ordinary Life

If only the heavy pain I say to you
were less real than our bodies that feel joy.
I see your howling face
articulate with suicide
tear from my mind
with one last lash of pride
that white terrified horse,
"*You're not a man!*"
He hears!  He who had heard
with his thrilled face the click
of new bone within her cool womb,
he hears and wakes into the ordinary life.

They live a daily life:
all rage fused to one sweet flowering tree
that slowly sails on their stone boat
going down to glory.

# Anne

On the bed's edge,
everything rolled down now,
the heavy arms, shoulders, cooling—
her breast warm on her thigh,
the stretchmarks breathing. . . .
She was aware then, her knees opening, closing—
the chafings, the damp inner-folds, bruises—
their room dank with her smoking, locked;
four o'clock, the children sleeping. . . .
She was aware, toes clenched on the soiled garments,
the diaphragm pressing, rubbing,
was aware, a hand between her legs, holding, she
beyond his numb loneliness of words, there,
touching herself, musing, breathing her fingers, biting,
a girl-child trembling on a shoulder. . . .
And that evening, the dishes done,
wearing now a plain black dress,
there to the river's wide place
she came, where the ice was thin,
she, a country beauty,
and there went in.

# The Moment of No Recovery

It's quiet there.
The clock can barely move
its holy arms.
The name of that gazing
virgin's face
is gone.
It was not clever,
nothing there
was clever.
Everywhere
but in her sly,
softening face
the good elation
is over.
It is not at all
symptomatic
that on this
tangible wall
in June she sees
one sailboat
on a lake of roses.
Sailboat, I think
I'm old enough
to be simple.

Great is the honoring
of Father and Mother.
I was drowning, I was
drowning, with my wings.

# A Good Death

Father of Concord, the war comes!
Beautiful blue children call in the eastern field
bird songs? wave after wave? and forever?
If the world could be like him and sing,
if I could build my naked fear into that ecstasy
as Henry once could do and sigh,
or walk among the sad Waldens of the west
where love evolves that sweet face
called The Seasons. . . . All men must lie.
Like inborn gentleness they find
humiliation and then art.
A real life? A pond of simple reasons?
The smile changing to taste the dark?
The deep lake within the ordinary woman you lost?

If Henry sang like this to sing,
all rising from his loneliness to spring,
then no more excuses. The brave dream on.
The sleeping soldier smiles in the rain,
"a good death, a good death. . . ."
The world was born four billion years before.

# Song

And so I stopped myself to play:
Black bells on the river,
Small candles on the barges far away—
These new women deep inside my mind
I had to have. Goodbye girls!
It's been a lovely time.
Morning would not have the world this way.
It's time to go. The sweet air makes me weep.
End high: "to hear, to touch, to kiss, to die,
With thee again in sweetest sympathy."

# Blue Roses

May I
wait
on your
stoop?

Mine is
never
in the sun-
shine.

I'm not much
to look
at:

Poems be
my body of
shining.

# Arthur's Moon

Now with his stiff back
and both shoulders
my father holds up
the binoculars.

A great night
on the terrace.

Boy, look at that moon!
Look at that moon!
It looks like it's right
on top of us.

# Songs for Paul Blackburn

### 1

The girl's dark face frowns,
"the ship is almost out of sight."
She bites her watch, chin on her
city-soft hands. "The water has calmed
down now." Yawns, smiles, embarrassed
she sees me, turns away.
"Look at the *boat*, Dad."
The milk-blue rock-flowers
of the cresting wake,
tiny blooms of glee.

### 2

The very small freighter moves low in the sea
beside our white ship, a froth of milk aft,
simple pale clouds motionless in the deep
planes above the bow. It is slower
with its weight of grain and single engine.
Slowly it falls behind us toward
the inexpressibly perfect sun: golden bridge,
red shining hull, and the tall blue stack.
I can look back on it now. Its captain
and crew are invisible and magical to me

as we sail closer to the sea
of the ancient Greeks. I will
still see its flag.


3


As I write quietly the men and women sleep
in bunks beside me. I stir. I press the pillows
deeply to uncover the fresh, wet faces
of my friends. They are all the way up here
drifting where I stand, their strange human
words tucked over them. Their life
is not sweet. I read for them.
We are all sailing too far.


4


The surface water moves with the wind,
changes from winter to spring,
knows the moon and sun,
knows living man and woman.
In the deep water there is
no star, no day.
It is night without end.
It is like the black of space
that is the natural light of our universe.

# Inscription

Now Sonia dreams, tired of her heavy body
and the sun. She smiles and is young.
How cool here in this shade
under the ancient arch and pre-Christian wall.
The sand floor is fine in my hand.

I move to her bench recently placed for rest.
We look together through the sun-filled door and steps.
I follow up the stairwell, and she is wise.
Here we can see the whole Nabatean city
from its sunrise to its paradise.

"Lord, help your servant Nilus,
the builder of this place
and his children."
O good wife, it is a boulevard
we're walking down.

*from*

# The Grand Concourse
*(1990)*

# Thanks Forever

Look at those empty ships
floating north
between south-running ice
like big tulips
in the Narrows
under the Verrazano
toward the city harbor.
I'm parked here,
out of work all year.
No hurry now
and sleep badly.
But I'm self-employed.
My new job's
to wave them in.
Hello freighter,
hello tanker.
Welcome, welcome,
to New York.

# Extreme Love

Lady, resting
to practice the walker,
pink robe charming
and mandarin,
lace leaves
under shy buttons—
she waits, sleeps,
her shaved head
crayoned purple
for the x-ray.
"You're lucky,
your majesty.
You have a new
young soldier
to walk with today."

We're coming back now:
one sweating, one shivering.
Oh how excited we get
just going around a few steps.

# Waxwings

O three-toned green little place with trees,
with toy-red chimneys, one frosted, one blowing,
with tractor, toolshed, tumbling barn,
with a pink curtain in the girl's window.

O men in millhats shovel and talk,
snow so deep the cattle seem yellow.
"Out, out," the housecat flies
into the sizzling surprise.

Then waxwings snip the wick of day,
supper's good and wood is dry,
headboards hum as freight goes by.
Next morning, up and back,
every fencepost wears a cap.

# Finding Peace

I see that my father
feels smaller and weaker.
He looks at his feet
as he finds our way,
and his hands are fragile
making a point,
the sky too strong
behind his sunglasses.
In fact, everything is too big
on him, his sleeves and pants
and robe. He is as small as my daughter
on her toes when he goes to kiss her.
We walk slower, and I choose
not to go too far
and the argument not so serious
as before or as long.
But when we sit, upstairs,
and his cigar is lit, his authority
hurts me still, wonderful
and never wrong. "The old time doctors
were more devoted," he says.
And each time now we speak
of cemeteries, the empty
family plot of four.
This week of Rosh Hashana he went
to visit his father's grave and
his tiny mother, Bella. He sat
on one of the stone benches.

"It was beautiful," he said,
"very peaceful." And he admired
the way the name was still so fresh
and perfectly carved: "Kessler."
I told him that he was lucky. A poet
could give a man immortality.
And such was his son.
"In death you find peace, they say."
Today, on the boardwalk, I sensed
this fear in me.

# Ballad for Dave

Driving south in sleet
I know you're coming north.
Take it easy son,
whatever road you're on.

Hope the old car's safe.
Pray you stay awake.
Take it easy son,
whatever road you're on.

Watch the ice at Great Bend.
Gear down in the dark.
Take it easy son,
whatever road you're on.

Don't pass trucks downhill.
Keep the music off.
Stay away from ghosts.
Stay away from thoughts.

Something sees us both
turning toward our town.
Take it easy son,
whatever road you're on.

# The Friday Night Life

And when you came home from work not having gone out
with the girls to worship Friday night at the bar
and I was upstairs in bed listening to music
and you said how great I looked in my jeans
and brown checked shirt
and I urged you to sit next to me
and I kissed you for the first time in months
and you didn't turn away right away
and your legs were open in their slacks
and I smiled
and kissed you again sweetly tenderly like
the immature person I am
and there was no hate in you
and I felt the miracle of the realness
and the humor in us
and kissed you on the neck where your curls
are bleached by marriage like mine
and still the same because I've always loved
your scented body
and on the lips and cheeks again then innocently gently
you got up disengaging
and said amazingly flirtatiously now be patient
you can't just barge in
and went glowing downstairs to make Sabbath
for the family
and I thought it was happening
and I was in my place
and everything was in its place.

# Sun

Sun, I'm happy to see you.
I'm a small child who has had pain and fear.
Now it's over for awhile and I'm grateful
for your company.

Come up. Cover my day with your glory,
and I will play at immortality.

# Grand Concourse

1

Mommy
when I first met her

had the softest
sweetest face

you've ever seen
in this world.

2

You know what I mean. The dead call us.
Come on, they say, why waste your time on living.

3

You could live here hundreds of years.
It wouldn't be enough to live here a lifetime.

4

Thought doesn't matter, he says to himself, shaving,
only to be here with them for as long as you can,

recognizable.


5

Look at this chair.
Have you ever seen a greater chair than that?

It could be in a museum.
It could last a thousand years.


6

Holidays coming on.  Her 87th birthday passes.  No presents
    or visits,
except for Doris, on the 3rd floor, who takes her shopping,
sits with her in the park and has a bitter, miserly husband.


7

It's the first real beach of the year.
Look at all the people here.

8

She's off to work, perhaps the last first day back after
     25 years.
Later, her face and small shoulders calm at the kitchen
     table,
standing, reading the bills, choice and charge ahead
and a classroom of new girls and boys.


9

The small dog exits
lowly barking
right
and left
before
stepping out.


10

Who's drinking tea?
Are you drinking it inside or should I bring it out?

Look at how smooth the street sounds.

The best times are at night when we sit
in our bathrobes, read and talk.

11

In that house
we could have
looked out
over the world.

In this house
we're buried
with the rest.


12

I see you're dressed up today, she said.
No, these are my usual clothes, he said.
I tucked my shirt in, that's all.
It's the way I am. I just have
a dressed up look.

A dressed up look, she said, leaving.
See you later, he said, smiling.


13

A howling kid running crazy,
hanging onto a garbage cracker,
a piece of a parent.

14

At dinner, after Yom Kippur and walk,
she spoke:
        "I want to make a speech.
        I want to thank you
        for being good to me.
        You always tried
        to do your best
        when I . . ."
Then she said,
        "can't go on,"
        and stopped.


15

In sentences, a teenager tells of his experience in a group
being trained for their own dying.
Weeks later he is informed his brain tumor
was a mistake, and he must go.

He left sadly
and never went home.

He joined the army
and paints barracks.

16

She went with a group to Jay Street,
a concert of retired musicians
brought together by the Union.

The bus was very clean, she says.
We had stacks of sandwiches and fresh coffee.

The day cost one dollar.


17

It's good
to breathe here
on Simhat Torah.

Who knows about
tomorrow's hospital.

New front steps.
A street to read by.
Eyes for gratitude.

18

I did what I could
I did what I could.

Right, during those years
we did what we could.


19

I'm much older now and no threat to anyone.
So let's be quiet and talk.


20

All musicians share
        the same
                obscurity.

Give up

        and pick up
your horn.

21

Our mothers are rooming together in Florida.
Our fathers are in their arks of earth.
Our children are in their worlds and work.


22

He was the most brilliant man, she says.
When he would order boots for the boys
you had to show him the skins from the animal
and he would choose the best.

# God's Cigar

And the fire took your thousand packages in rubber bands
that was my legacy in closet and drawer
and the socks from the thirties and forties with clocks
and fifty-five years of paid-in-full receipts
and leases to ancient apartment houses
and butts of pocket pencils older than mummies
and erasers like the nosenubs of pharaohs
and the twin temples of humidor and shoeshine box
and the forest of ash hangers and cedar shoetrees
and on the altar of the chifforobe
the fire ate like Uneeda Biscuits
the paper-framed gallery of children's children
and your father's vest of landlord's keys
and your mother Bella's humor in his fur collar
and after the fire your leg *brent* from your first fall
  on cement
the whole continent of Africa infected into your calf
that had run the tracks of old New York
a shin no graft or hand could cover
yet you run to the bank on the first Oh my master
your dime harder to borrow than a million from Chase
leg of the second nephew of Harris Mandelbaum
  peddlar millionaire
leg of the science scholar erased by the quota
leg of the four A.M. lunch at the 33rd Street Automat
leg of the hundred yard olympics at McCombs Park
a body no doctor had corrupted in forty-five years

no needle had tasted no clavicle lung x-rays
but what have you got my father my pal
but a chair in a bathtub
and a garbage pail to rinse and *daven* over
this Litvak baby leg that played in the park in Mariampol
where the Mandelbaums made black breads for the Czar's army
and saved their men conscription or self-mutilation.
And those who only have eyes for the tinsel of the
   ideological angel
what do you make of such a man
that kinky haired sprinter on Rockaway Beach Boulevard
see him now with his limb of drenched bandages
flying in front of buses
Without wings.

# Anniversary Gift (August 24, 1979)

Affection and admiration
step out across the hayed and buzzing field
which belongs to no one, common pasture.
He slightly shorter than she, both over fifty-sixty,
from distant cities, working together in the empire,
sky eloquent with every cloud, yet no storm.

See now they've reached the dark friction of the forest line
and turn left toward the pond-path where the white cabin
faces the mountain. He's an actor, she an actress,
just like us. And there they wander from our fantasy
of their intention. Yellow wildflowers call them over
the equator of the wheatfield to the place where we all
watched one sunset a summer-coated russet fox with her
two leaping pups snatch a thousand crickets for supper.

And here they come rounding close and wave as they
promenade sweetly talking with mutual tone and gesture
as the wind jumps, doors clap, the earth's drum blasts
the baby clouds. We stumble from our stoops and stores
and join our stage friends in Pompeii and Herculaneum
who know best how to enjoy the mellowness of an illusion.

:

And that evening in the sky:
Father has milk and milk-bread before bed
sitting at his small white table.

Momma looks more at the apartment lights
above her covers and the dark stores.

Wife puts her glasses on the famous face of her book
shuts the toy lamp and listens to the fan.

Daughter sees her own beauty move in thoughts
of summer work and walls of spring flowers.

Big boy forgets to put away his bike
and falls asleep with his saxophone.

Dog, sunned and hugged all day,
finds fresh water and a nice chair.


:


The records show that somebody named
    H. Propidius Celsinus
paid for the rebuilding of the Temple of Isis after the
earthquake of 62. The joke is he was only six. Actually,
his father, a slave, bought his free son a seat in the Ordo.
If not for the eruption of 79 this kid Celsinus would have
been Chief Magistrate of Pompeii. It all stopped on our
wedding anniversary, one thousand nine hundred years ago.


:

Love, death is everywhere, life just right here.
Dreamthings like us must live by laws of kindness.
"There are good days and there are fair days."
Well, how's that? What do you think of it?
I made this whole thing by myself, and all I want from
you is slower and lighter and higher and tighter and deeper
  and smoother
and faster and gentler. Let's make lunch together.
I kiss your forehead curls.

# Zero

The Ch-ing Emperor's troupe of buried horses
The visor-blinded horses of the jousts
The pompadoured bronze horses of the Renaissance
The Elgin horses roped and dragged from Athens
The Generalissimo's mount in Freedom Square
The noble cheval burst by English archers
The cannon deaf cavalry of Bull Run
The Imam's arabians writhing on the cross of Allah
The dive-bombed horse with tongue of broken glass
Siegfried's horror horse with Panzer lancer
Horses were never interested in war
War no longer interested in horses
The investment stallions seeding twitched mares
The ground horse catfood of the dispossessed
The cast horses in the mafia stables
The shiver brained coursers wearing buttercups
The cossack horses higher than whole villages
The porcelain dancers of the Lippizaner
The Indian ponies trained to die like savages
The slipping horsefeet of Alexander Nevsky
The heart-horned horses of the picadores
The cigarette horses branded sex and death
The pinup stallions of gold college girls
The cowboy's true horse on the lonely range
The dawn is the head of a sacrificed horse

# Right Now

I see children with faces unraveling into balls of shreds
  of cries.
I see children whose fathers are specks of disappearing
  red dust.
I see children eaten by the president's Dracula-smirk
  helicopter-armpit wave.
I see children whose parents sell them away to strangers
  for a buck
or bucket of plastic chicken because you have to sell or
  sacrifice.
I see children wetnursed by minimum-wage slaves.
I see fetuses punished as if they were senile
  grandfathers.
I see children hugging their crumbling parents who hang
  on their tiny clavicles,
huge smothering dolls stuffed with the poisons of the
  time.
I see children shot by accident and backed over by
  accident
and failed by accident and falling out of windows by
  accident
and robbed off the streets too small standing to reach the
  deranged hand
of some American citizen with a velour sofa for a car.
I see children drowning suicided on white powder in gift
  condos.
Check high school public drug telephone at 68th and 2nd.
I see children whose male adult is every booze violent

knock on the door.

I see children iron masked by assistant principals.

I see children scanned by the lewd blue monocular of network TV.

I see geniuses packing immortal bags full of grocery
insecticides.

I see the terror at the locked school door and the
doorless school toilet.

I see shy children restrained for singing to themselves.

I see children fire-bombed to death by the police of
Philadelphia.

I see boarder babies shrieking for every mammal's rights.

I see college infants auctioned into sports by born again
elders.

I see children chained by corpse parents insane after a
week of worthless work.

I see tiny human hands and feet laced with hell roaches
and lead.

I see movies vomiting reels of rat-perfed frames of
demon-children.

Beat the fear of God into them. Scare the devil out of them.

Crack babies scream and scratch.

Twelve year old wives too undeveloped to drive the
shotgun pickup.

Fetuses fished out on educational TV.

Infants living alone with a telephone.

I see baby-porn selling tires and A.T. & T.

I see right now in central New York, a boy of ten walking
miles alone

to the cancer corridor, his mother's only visitor.

And then what, America, and then what?

# Plain Poplar

And he said, "Fuck you, fuck you," he said. "You're no good."
And I said, "Bullshit, you're full of shit," I said.
And he came over his body shaking with violated
                                    commandment
and raised his spotted smoky fist and said,
                                    "I'm going to do
something you won't like if you say that,"
                                    and I smirked at 220,
and was afraid of my father's great trembling,

                    and he was "1898," Oh Lord,
            he was 98 pounds,
        and he raised his fist on
                            his breast
                                    bone,

        and after went in
                and put his arm over his eyes,

    and I saw it, my God,
                and it was no one else I saw

but the strength of my Pop.

And, yes, he set his paper down and raised his fist again.

Oh washed facebrow unfrozen on a sill of poplar,
no make-up, a man a man, your perfect silver curls,

moist under the shroud, is the beauty of my father,

and I reached in

and touched your fist
again.
"Oh Dad is dead, Mom, Dad is dead."
And he got up from his chair
stiff and true
after I said, "bullshit,"

and he came
all wind in his shirt
and wet pants
and sour twenty dollar bills

and acid rubber bands and pencils
and brought his quick fist

reflexes snapping
in my bewildered, joyous eyes,
his fist
all taped, cracked

and cigar elegant,
his back

arced

as the Jewish prince he was,
                    "Just call me Artie."

And "Fuck you," he said, "fuck you."
        "You always take your mother's side."
                    And he came
            right over at 87
        and cash,
                gelt,
                    that was it,


    "You're a miser, I said, "You think poor."
"You're full of shit," he said.
            "Get a housekeeper," I said.
            "I'd rather jump
                        out the window," he said.


            "Dad is dead, Mom,
            Dad is dead,"

God damn it, Dad.
            Your eyes right to pegs
                    where the box closed,

        and your chest bones
                        peaceful
                and proud
        and strong.

Pow Pop! Pow Pop!

And his mouth made
"I love you I love you."
"Soon I will take a trip
on a train." (smile)
"Maybe tomorrow it will be better," (smile)
"a little better," (smile)
"a little better," (smile).

O Pop, who will curse your newspaper now?
"Why don't you ever wear a suit?" he said
"What kind of a man are you?" he said.
What a shot, Pop, what a shot.
Pow Pop! Pow Pop!

# South Bronx Chekhov

Out of the hall closet she offered the ties again for free,
stained, wrinkled, faded, wide as the depression,
moldy as their owners' last mattresses.
They're ugly and filthy, I said.
What corpse did you rip them off of?
So you don't want them, she said,
storing them back with shy steps,
her beautiful merchandise.
Why didn't I just accept them?
Why did I retract the bones in my arm?
Why didn't I extend a kind wing?
Why didn't I take them on my wings and do some business?